# Alexander
# GLAZUNOV

# VIOLIN
# CONCERTO
## Op. 82
### (1904)

## Study Score
### Partitur

PETRUCCI LIBRARY PRESS

# ORCHESTRA

2 Flutes
Piccolo
2 Oboes
2 Clarinets
2 Bassoons

4 Horns
2 Trumpets
3 Trombones

Timpani
Triangle
Cymbals
Glockenspiel
Harp

Violins I
Violins II
Violas
Violoncellos
Double Basses

Duration: ca. 20 minutes

First performance
St. Petersburg: February 15, 1905
Leopold Auer (violin solo)
Russian Musical Society Orchestra, Alexander Glazunov (conductor)

ISBN: 978-1-60874-139-7
This score is a slightly modified unabridged reprint of the score
issued in the mid-20th century by Muzgiz (State Music Publishers).
The score has been scaled to fit the present format.

Printed in the USA
First Printing: August, 2014

# VIOLIN CONCERTO

## Op. 82

### 1904

Alexander Glazunov (1865-1936)

# PETRUCCI LIBRARY PRESS

3
Cl.(B)
Fag.
I
V-no solo
3
Archi
6
Cl.(B)
Fag.
I
V-no solo
6
arco
p
arco
p
Archi
arco
p
arco
p

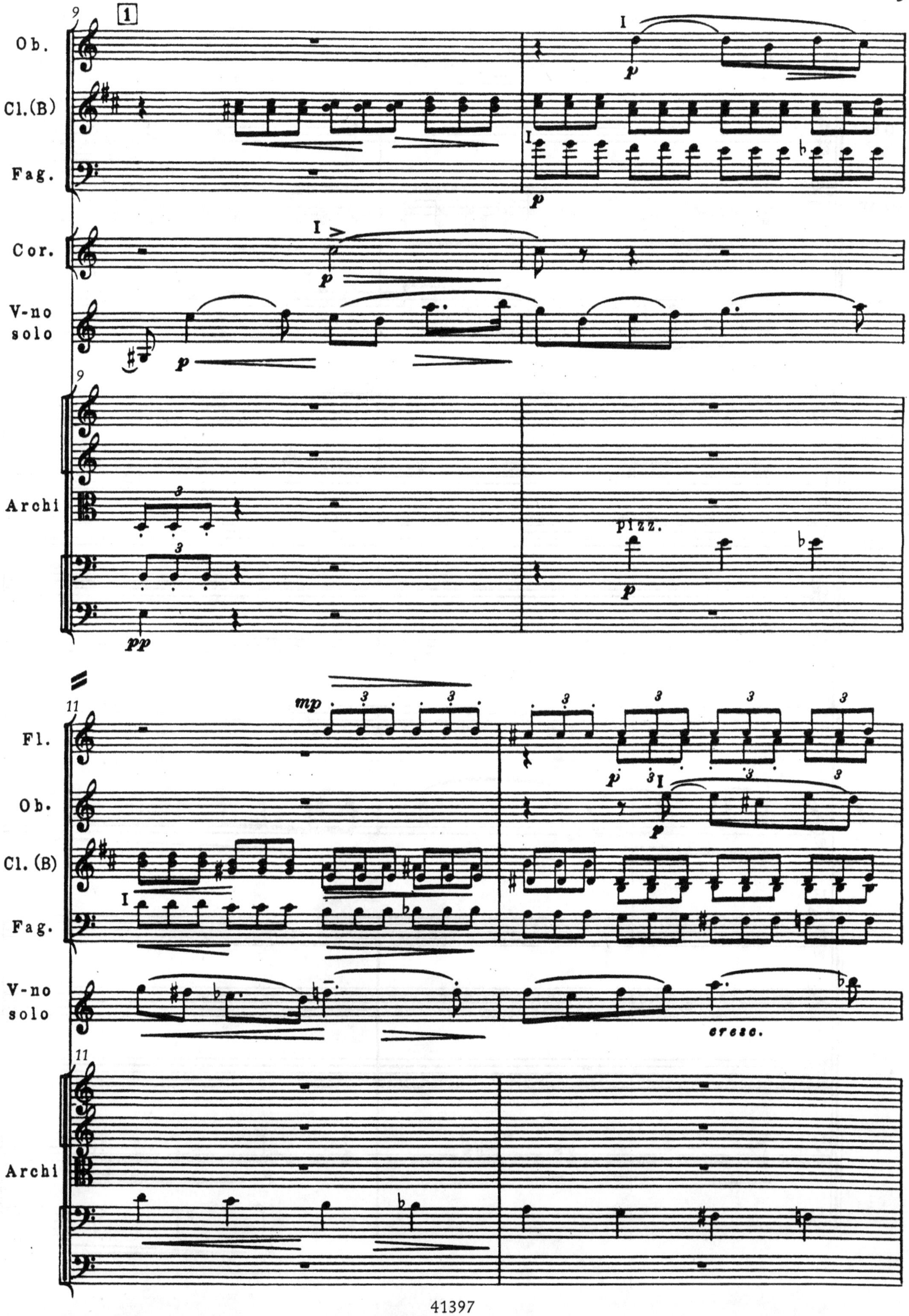
1
Ob.
Cl.(B)
Fag.
Cor.
V-no solo
Archi
pizz.
Fl.
cresc.

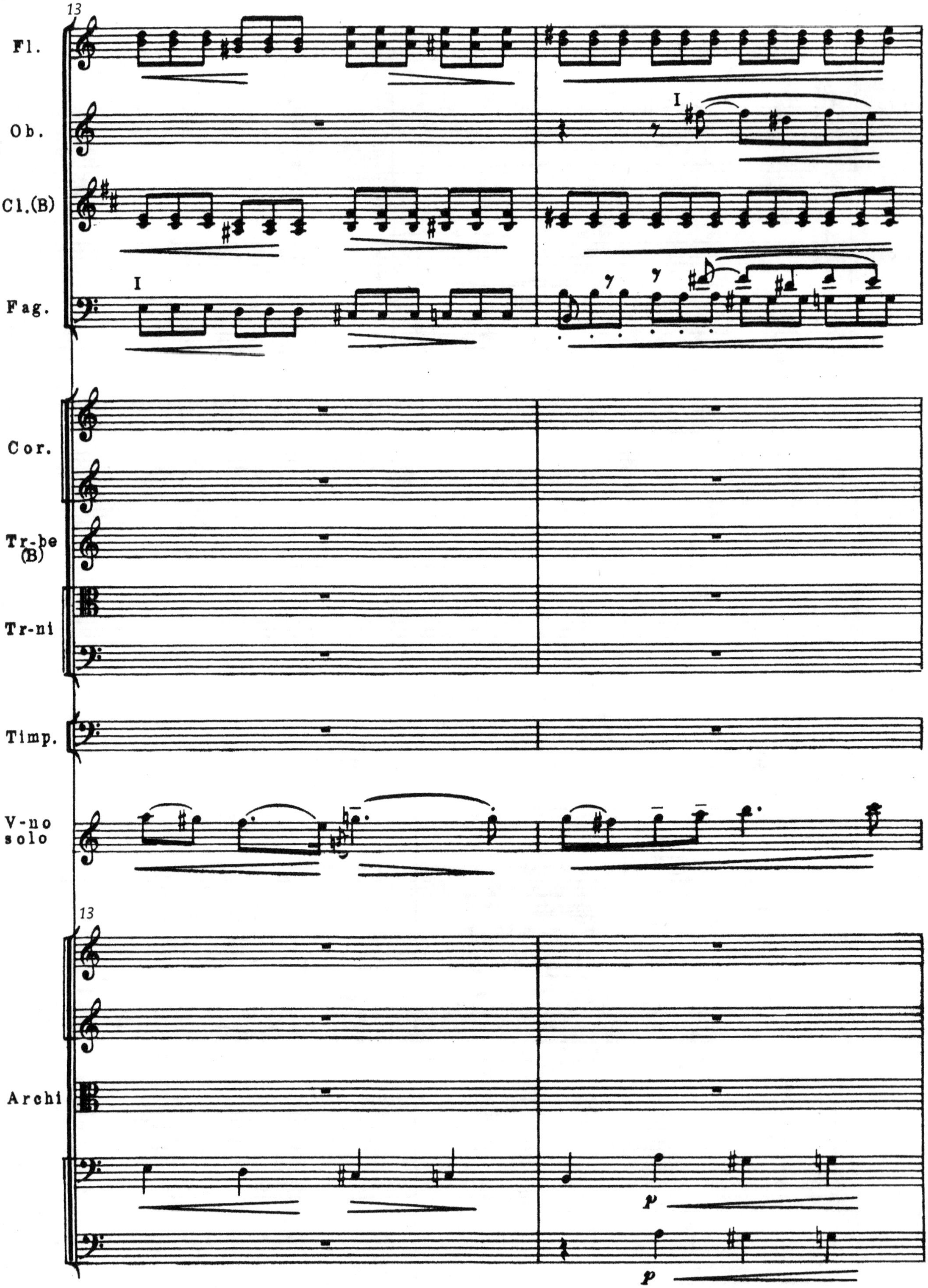
13
Fl.
Ob.
I
Cl.(B)
Fag.
I
Cor.
Tr-be (B)
Tr-ni
Timp.
V-no solo
13
Archi
p
p

15
Fl.
mf
Ob.
p
Cl. (B)
espr.
Fag.
I
Cor.
Tr-be (B)
Tr-ni
Timp.
V-no solo
f
Archi
p espr.

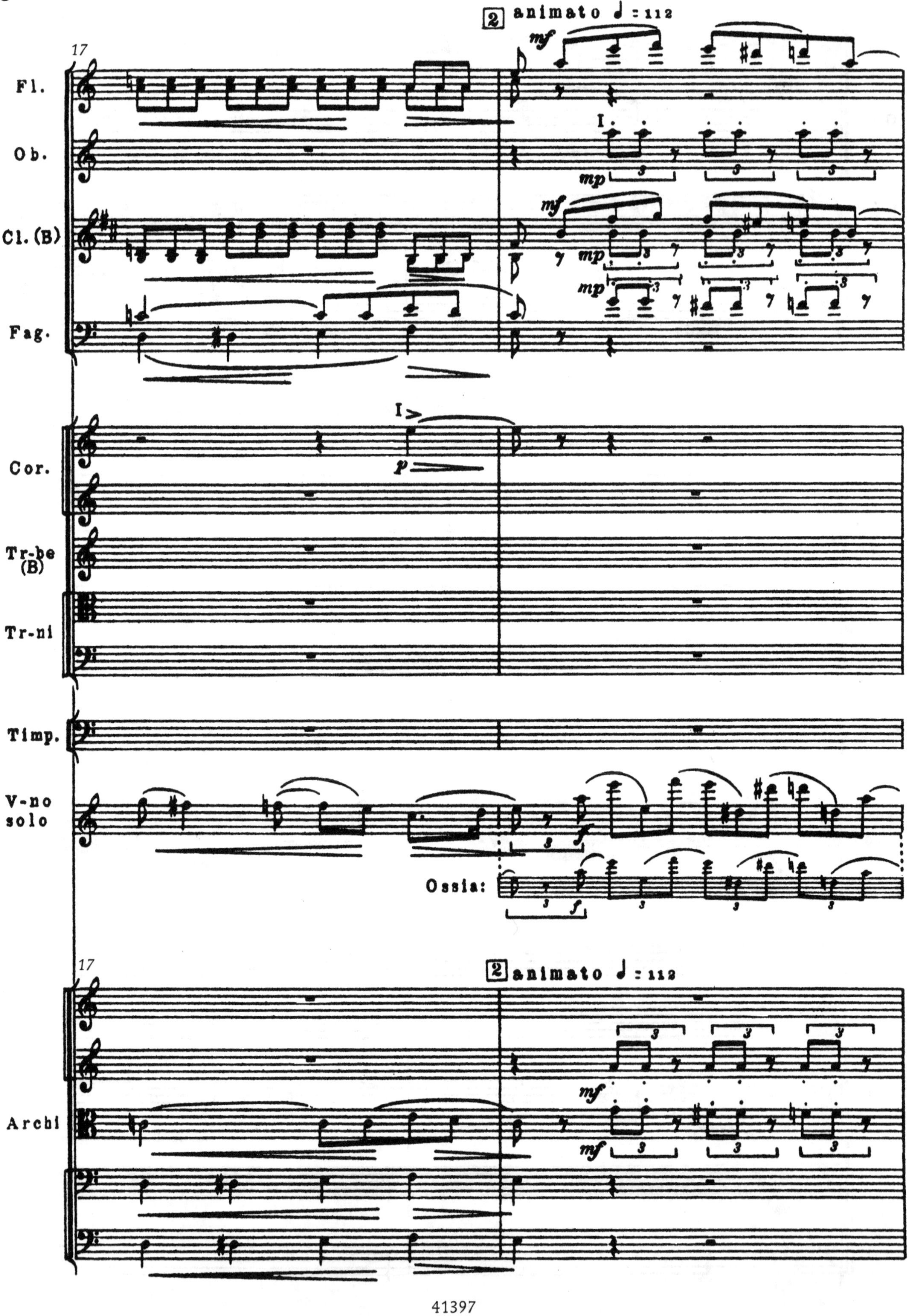
17
2 animato ♩ = 112
Fl.
Ob.
Cl. (B)
Fag.
Cor.
Tr-be (B)
Tr-ni
Timp.
V-no solo
Ossia:
Archi
mf
mp
p
f
I.

19
Fl.
Ob.
Cl.(B)
Fag.
Cor.
Tr-be (B)
Tr-ni
Timp.
V-no solo
etc.
Archi
mf
arco
mp

calando
riten.
3
a tempo
Cl. (B)
Fag.
V-no solo
Archi
arco
Fl.
Ob.
V-ni I
V-ni II
V-le
V-c.
espr.

32
Fl.
I
Ob.
Cl.(B)
Fag.
Cor.
mp
dim.
V-no solo
a piacere
mf
dim.
Archi
pizz.
p
4 tranquillo
37
V-no solo
p dolce
p
Archi
p
p espr.
mf
3

43
animando
I
rall.
Ob.
Cl.(B)
Cor.
V-no solo
Archi
mf
mp
pizz.
45
5
a tempo
animando
Fag.
cresc. poco
p
cresc.
arco
espr.

51
calando
Fl.
Cl.(B)
Fag.
V-no solo
Archi
mp
mf I
mp
mf
f
dim.
mf
dim.
arco
p
55
riten.
6 a tempo
Cl.(B)
Fag.
Cor.
I
V-no solo
Archi
p
cresc.
mf
mp
p dolce espr.
p cresc.
p cresc.
div.
espr.
arco

59
animando
Fl.
Ob.
Cl. (B)
Fag.
mf
Cor.
I
mf
Tr-be (B)
Tr-ni
Timp.
V-no solo
p
cresc.
59
animando
Archi
mf
pp cresc.
unis.

Più mosso ♩=120
62
7
Fl.
p
sf
Ob.
Cl.(B)
Fag.
Cor.
III
Tr-be (B)
Tr-ni
Timp.
V-no solo
f
10
3
11
62
7 Più mosso ♩=120
Archi

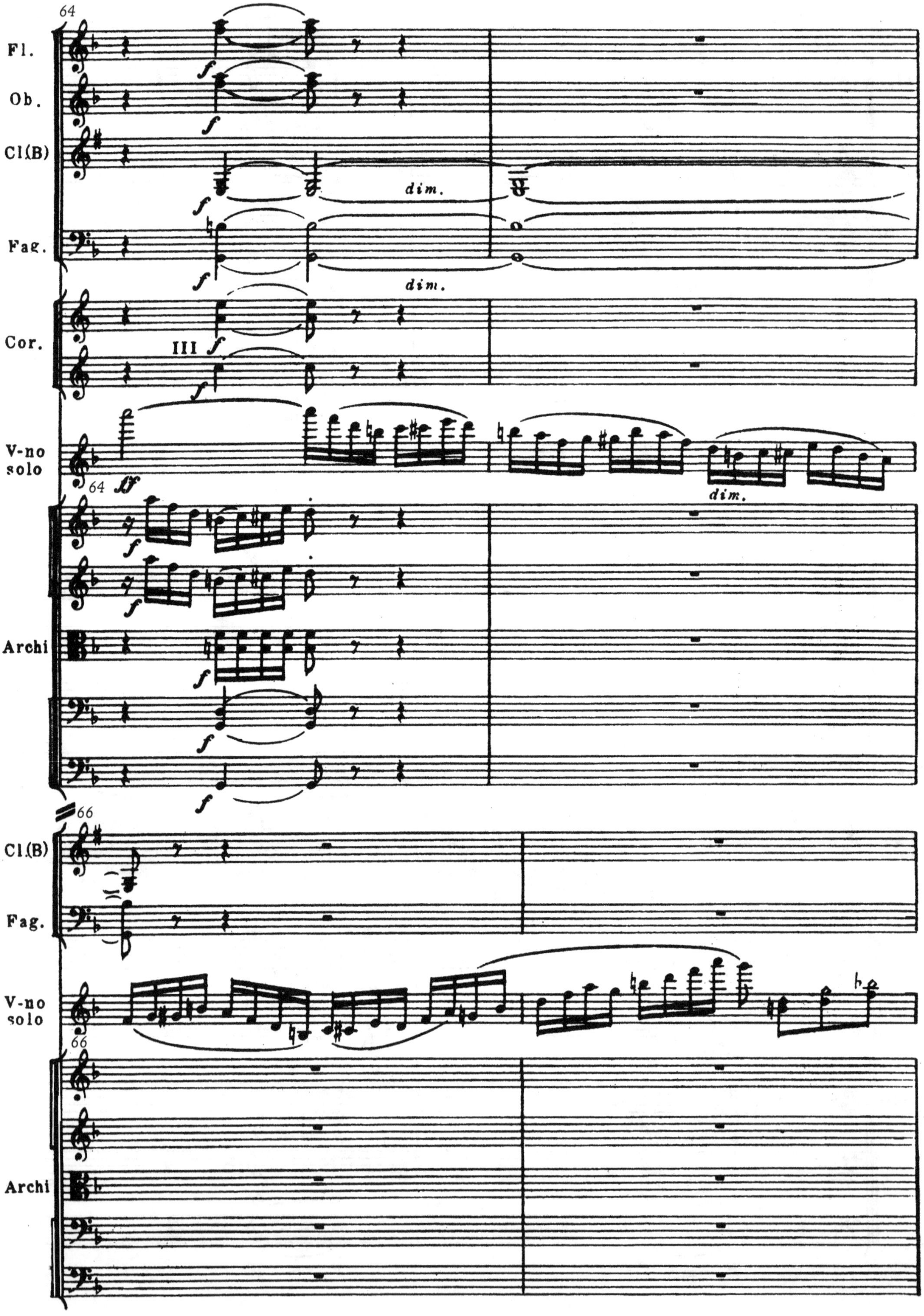
64
Fl.
Ob.
Cl.(B)
Fag.
Cor.
III
V-no solo
Archi
dim.
66

Tempo I
8
68
Picc.
Fl.
Ob.
Cl.(B)
Fag.
Cor.
Tr-be (B)
Timp.
Tr-lo
V-no solo
Archi
cresc.
pizz.
arco
(pizz.)
poco
(B)
I

71
Picc.
Fl.
Ob.
Cl.(B)
Fag.
Cor.
Tr-be
(B)
Timp.
Tr-lo
V-no
solo
Archi
II
I
dim.
p
mf
pp
tr
arco
div.

74
calando
Picc.
Fl.
Ob.
Cl.(B)
II
I
Fag.
I
p
pp
II
p
Cor.
III
p
p
Tr-be
(B)
Tr-ni
Timp.
74
calando
pp
pp
unis.
Archi
p espr.
pizz.
div. arco
mp
p
p
p espr.
pizz.
arco
mp
p
p

41397

80
9
Tranquillo ♩ = 76
Picc. muta in Fl.III
Picc.
solo
Fl.
II
Ob.
I
I solo
Cl.(B)
Fag.
Cor.
Tr-be (B)
Tr-ni
Timp.
Arpa
V-no solo
80
9 Tranquillo ♩ = 76
Archi
div.
dim
dim.
div. in 3
div.
dim.

22

41397

92
Fag.
I
mp
Arpa
mp
p
pp
V-no
solo
V-le
p espr.
pp
V-c.
div. in 3
pp
p espr.
p
2 C-b.
pizz.
pp
C-b.
p
pp
97
11
Fl.
II
mp
Cl.(B)
mp
p
Fag.
p
mp
Cor.
I
mp
p
cresc.
Arpa
p
cresc.
V-no
solo
cresc.
V-le
I.II unis.
V-c.
div. in 3
pizz.
p
cresc.
p

101
Fl.
Ob.
(Cl.II muta in A)
Cl.(B)
Fag.
Cor.
Tr-be (B)
Tr-ni
Arpa
V-no solo
f passionato
101
Archi
div.
sul D
div. in 3
arco
Tutti,div.
arco
pizz.

105
12
I.II
Fl.
Ob.
I
mp
Cl.(B)
mp
mf
p
Fag.
p
Cor.
p
Tr-be (B)
Tr-ni
Arpa
p
3
V-no solo
dolce
105
12
Archi
mp
mf
p
unis. pizz.
div.in3
pizz.
tutti pizz.

109
Fl.
III
p
cresc.
Ob.
I
Cl.(B)
Fag.
cresc
Cor.
I
Tr-be (B)
Tr-ni
Arpa
cresc.
V-no solo
cresc.
109
Archi
unis.
p cresc.
cresc.
cresc

112
Fl.
Ob.
I solo
Cl.(B)
I
Cl. (A)
II
Fag.
I
p espr.
Cor.
I
Tr-be (B)
Tr-ni
Arpa
V-no solo
più piano
112
div.
pizz.
div. arco
Archi
arco
div. pizz.
arco
div. arco
pizz.

28

41397

119
Fl.
Ob.
I
mp
Cl.(A)
II
Fag.
Cor.
Tr-be (B)
Tr-ni
Arpa
V-no solo
6
6
3
119
mp espr.
Archi

121
14
Fl.
Ob.
I
Cl.(A)
II
Cl. II muta in B
Fag.
Cor.
I
Tr-be (B)
Tr-ni
Arpa
gliss.
muta C, Dis, Es, Fis, Ges, A, His
V-no solo
121
Archi
unis. arco

123
Fl.
Arpa
dim.
V-no
solo
dim.
123
mf
p
div.
unis.
Archi
div.
dim.
pizz.
div.
dim.
pizz.
125
calando
I.II
Fl.
III
Arpa
V-no
solo
125
Archi

127
15
a tempo
Fl.
III
Ob.
Cl.(B)
I
Fag.
Cor.
III
Tr-be (B)
Tr-ni
Arpa
V-no solo
127
15
a tempo
Archi
unis. arco

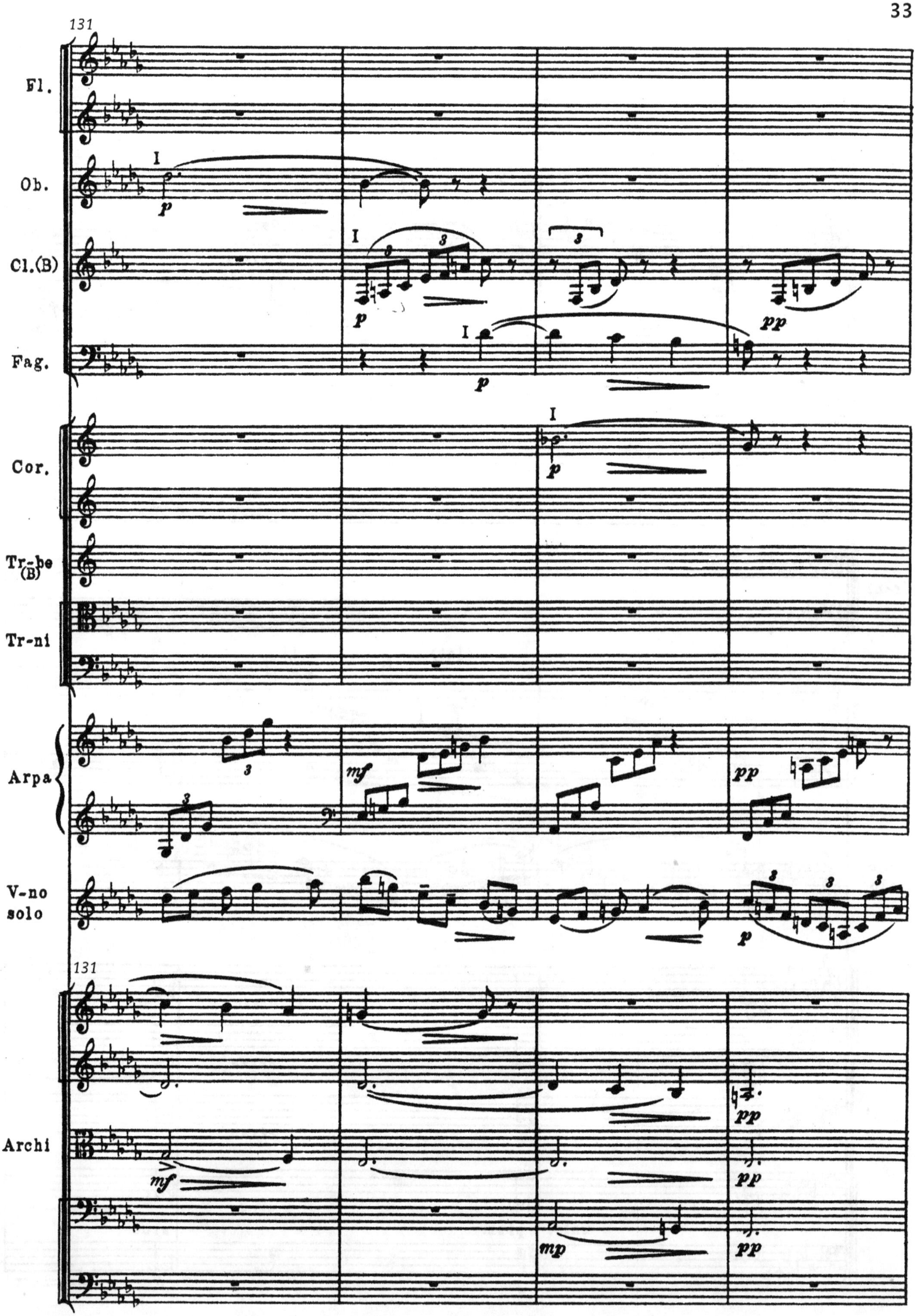
131
Fl.
Ob.
Cl.(B)
Fag.
Cor.
Tr-be (B)
Tr-ni
Arpa
V-no solo
131
Archi

135
Fl.
Ob.
Cl.(B)
Fag.
Cor.
Tr-be (B)
Tr-ni
Arpa
V-no solo
Archi
(la♮)
cresc.
unis.
pizz.
arco

16
138
Fl.
III
Ob.
Cl. (B)
Fag.
I
Cor.
IV
Tr-be
(B)
I muta in A
Tr-ni
Arpa
V-no
solo
più piano
16
138
Archi
pizz.
div. pizz.
arco
div.

141
Fl.
Ob.
I
Cl.(B)
Fag.
I
Cor.
III
Tr-be
Tr-ni
(la♮)
Arpa
(la ♮)
V-no
solo
141
div.
div.
Archi
arco
unis.

17
144
Fl.
III
Ob.
I
Cl. (B)
Fag.
Cor.
Tr-be
Tr-ni
Arpa
V-no solo
dim.
17
144
Archi
div.

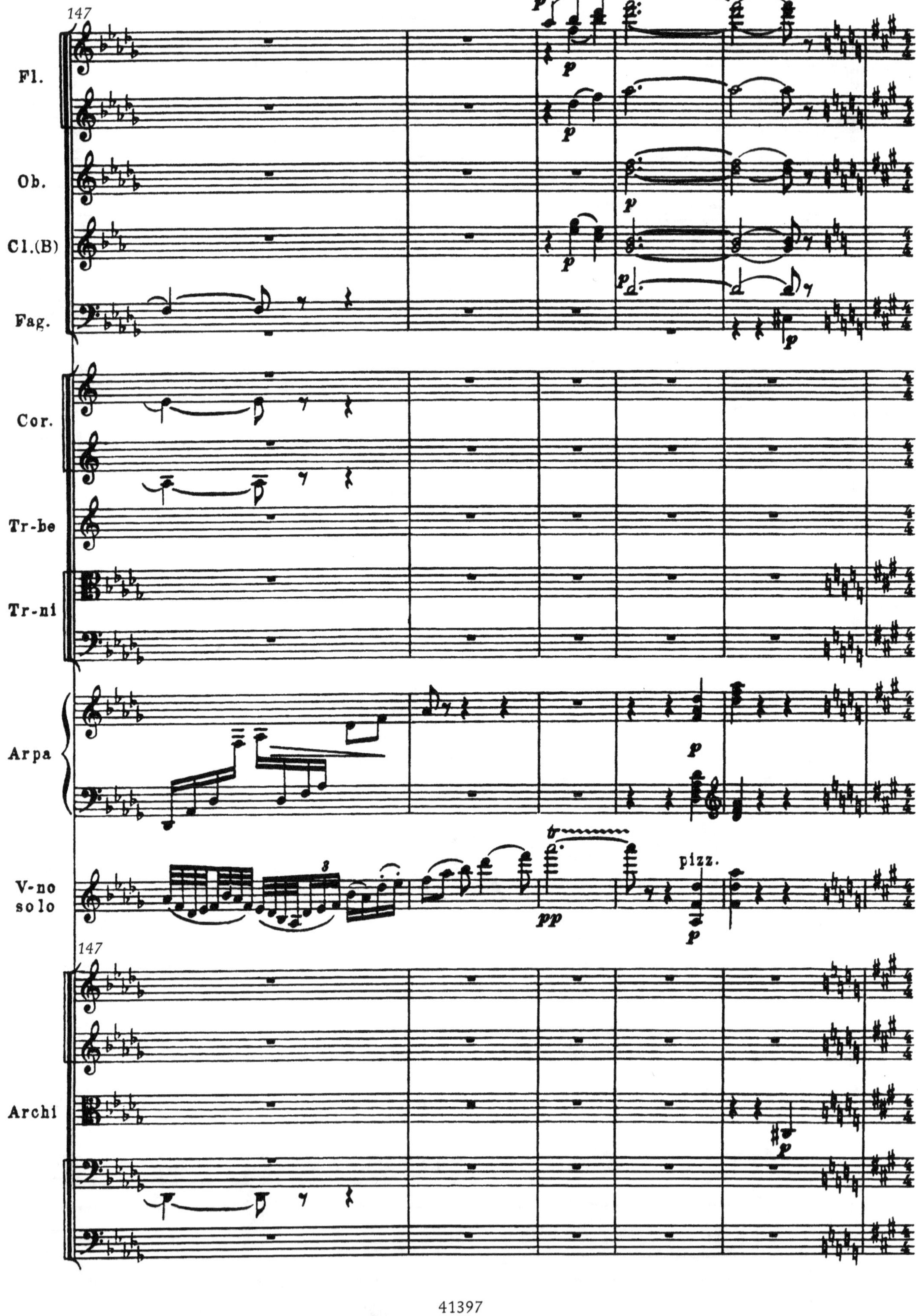
147
Fl.
Ob.
Cl.(B)
Fag.
Cor.
Tr-be
Tr-ni
Arpa
V-no solo
Archi
p
pp
pizz.

18
152
Tempo I
riten.
a tempo
Fl.
Ob.
Cl.(B)
Fag.
Cor.
Tr-be
Tr-ni
Archi
div.

riten.
157
Fl.
Ob.
Cl.(B)
Fag.
Archi
div.
unis. pizz.
a tempo
161
19
Cor.
unis.
sul A
III

riten. poco
riten. poco
165
Fl.
III
Ob.
I
Cl.(B)
Fag.
I
Cor.
I
165
V-ni I
V-ni II
div.
V-le
a tempo. Più animato ♩=112
20
168
Fl.
III
Ob.
I
Cl.(B)
muta in A
Cor.
I
V-no solo
arco
168
V-ni I
pizz.
V-ni II
pizz.
V-le
unis. pizz.

42

41397

174
Cor.
III
I
mp
V-no solo
174
(pizz.)
mp
Archi
176
21
Cl.(A)
mf
Cor.
I
(A) I
Tr-be
mp
V-no solo
mf
176
pizz.
mf
Archi

44

41397

22 pesante
182
I.II
Fl.
Ob.
Cl.(A)
Fag.
Cor
Tr-be (B)
(B)
Tr-ni
Timp.
V-no solo
Ossia:
p sub.
pesante
arco
div.
Archi

185
23
Fl.
p sub.
Ob.
p sub.
Cl.(A)
p sub.
I
mp
p sub. poco
Fag.
Cor.
p sub. poco
p sub. poco
Tr-be (B)
Tr-ni
tr
p poco
V-no solo
mf passionato
185
23
p sub.
p sub.
p
Archi
p sub.
p
p sub.
pp
p sub.
pp

188
Fl.
Cl(A)
Fag.
Cor.
V-no solo
188
Archi
colla parte
a tempo
190
Fl.
Ob.
Cl.(A)
Fag.
Cor.
V-no solo
190
div.
Archi
pizz.

192
24
Fl.
Ob.
Cl(A)
Fag.
Cor.
V-no solo
Archi
I
I.II
mf
p
mp
pizz.
arco
div.
div. arco
unis.
psaltando
194
segue

196
Fl.
Fag.
Cor.
V-no solo
Archi
mp
I
I.II
p
198
Cl.(A)
mf
p espr.
unis. arco
p saltando

200
25
animato
cresc.
Fl.
Ob.
Cl.(A)
Fag.
Cor.
Tr-be (B)
Tr-ni
V-no solo
Archi
pizz.
mf
f

202
Fl.
I
mf
Ob.
mf
Cl.(A)
mf
Fag.
mf
Cor.
p
Tr-be (B)
Tr-ni
V-no solo
202
mf
Archi

204
Fl.
Ob.
Cl.(A)
mf
Fag.
mf
Cor.
Tr-be
(B)
Tr-ni
V-no
solo
204
Archi
arco
mf
mf
mf

206
rall.
II
Fl.
Ob.
Cl.(A)
Fag.
Cor.
Tr-be
(B)
Tr-ni
V-no
solo
206
rall.
Archi
arco

209
II
Fl.
Ob.
I
mf
Cl.(A)
a2
p
Fag.
Cor.
Tr-be
(B)
Tr-ni
V-no
solo
Archi
arco
div.

212
26
Tranquillo
I solo
Fl.
Cl.(A)
I
Fag.
mf
V-no solo
sul G
dolce
212
pp
Archi
pp
unis.
mf
pp
mf
215
I
Fl.
Cl.(A)
I solo
p
I solo
Fag.
p
p
Cor.
I
p
V-no solo
215
p dolcissimo
dolcissimo
Archi
p
p

218
Cl.(A)
Fag.
Cor.
V-no solo
Archi
animando
sempre
sul G
mp
p
220
27
rall.
a tempo
Fl.
mf
pp

223
Fl.
Ob.
Cl.(A)
Fag.
I solo
Cor.
Tr-be (B)
Tr-ni
Timp.
V-no solo
sul D
223
Archi
dolciss.
dolciss.

226
animando
riten.
Fl.
II.III
Ob.
Cl.(A)
cresc.poco
Fag.
cresc.poco
Cor.
Tr-be (B)
Tr-ni
Timp.
V-no solo
sul G
cresc.
226
animando
riten.
cresc.poco
pizz.
Archi
sul D

a tempo
28
230
Fl.
I II
III
Fl. III muta in Picc.
Ob.
Cl.(A)
II
I
Fag.
Cor
Tr-be (B)
muta in A
Tr-ni
Timp.
V-no solo
8
Archi
arco

233
Fl.
Cl.(A)
Fag.
Cor.
CADENZA
V-no solo
a piacere
V-no solo
ten.
dim.
pizz.
più sost.
arco

257
p
259
261
262
dim.
263
264
265
dim.
265
29
266
animando
Cor.
mf
dim.
III
V-no solo
p
cresc.
f
V-c.
pp
cresc. poco
mp
C-b.

269
Cor.
III
solo
Timp.
V-no solo
dim.
269
V-c.
C-b.
30
(coperti)
273
III
dim.
cresc.
cresc. poco
276
cresc. poco

279
Cl.(A)
Fag.
V-no solo
V-c.
C-b.
dim.
281
Tr-be (A)
Timp.
sole
cresc.
p cresc.
283
31
Allegro ♩=♩.= 84
Cor.
marc.

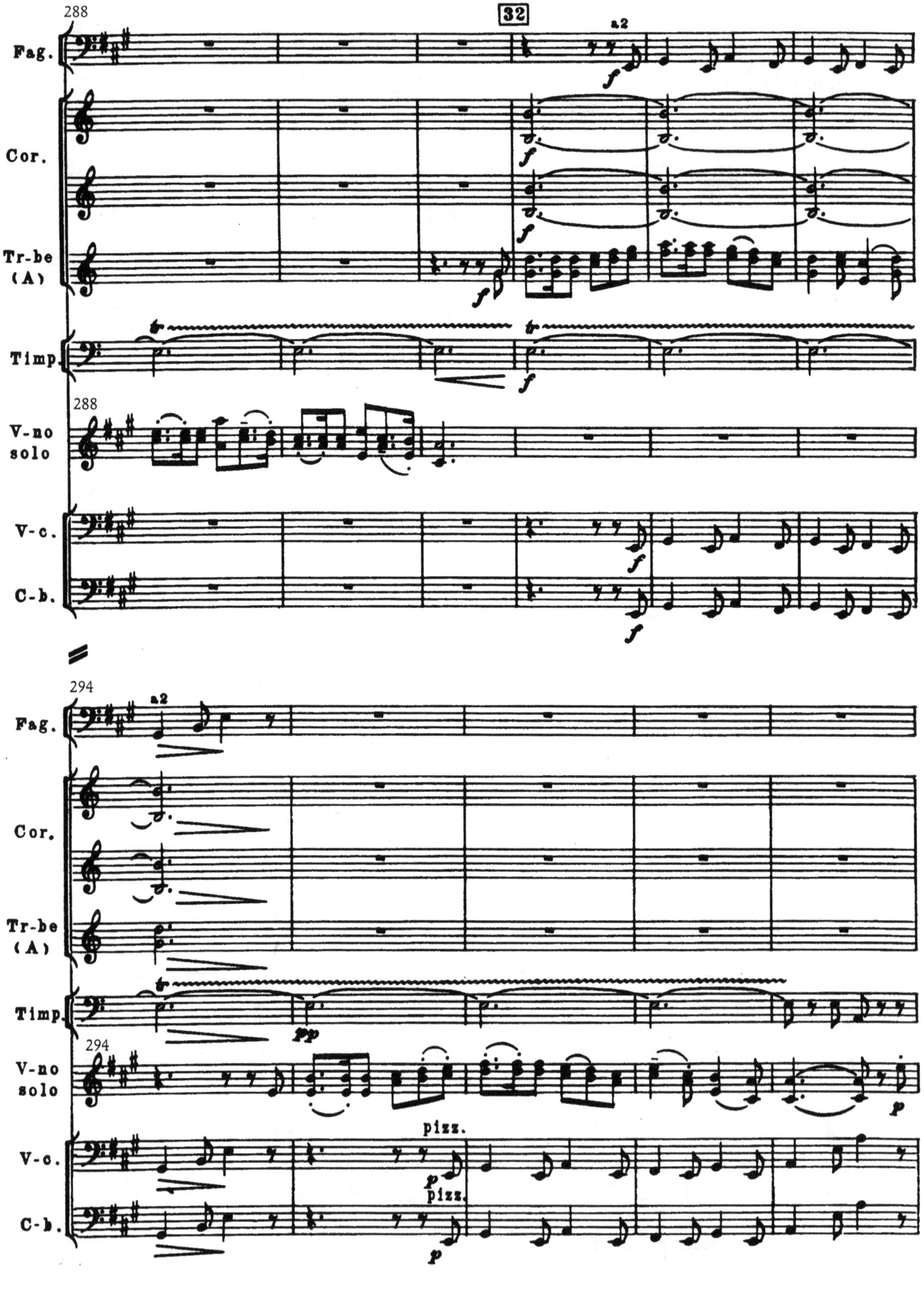
288
32
Fag.
a2
Cor.
Tr-be (A)
Timp.
tr
V-no solo
V-c.
C-b.
f
294
pp
pizz.
p

299
33
Ob.
I
pp
V-no solo
pizz.
p
Archi
302
Picc.
solo
Fl.
Cl.(A)
Tr-lo
Arpa

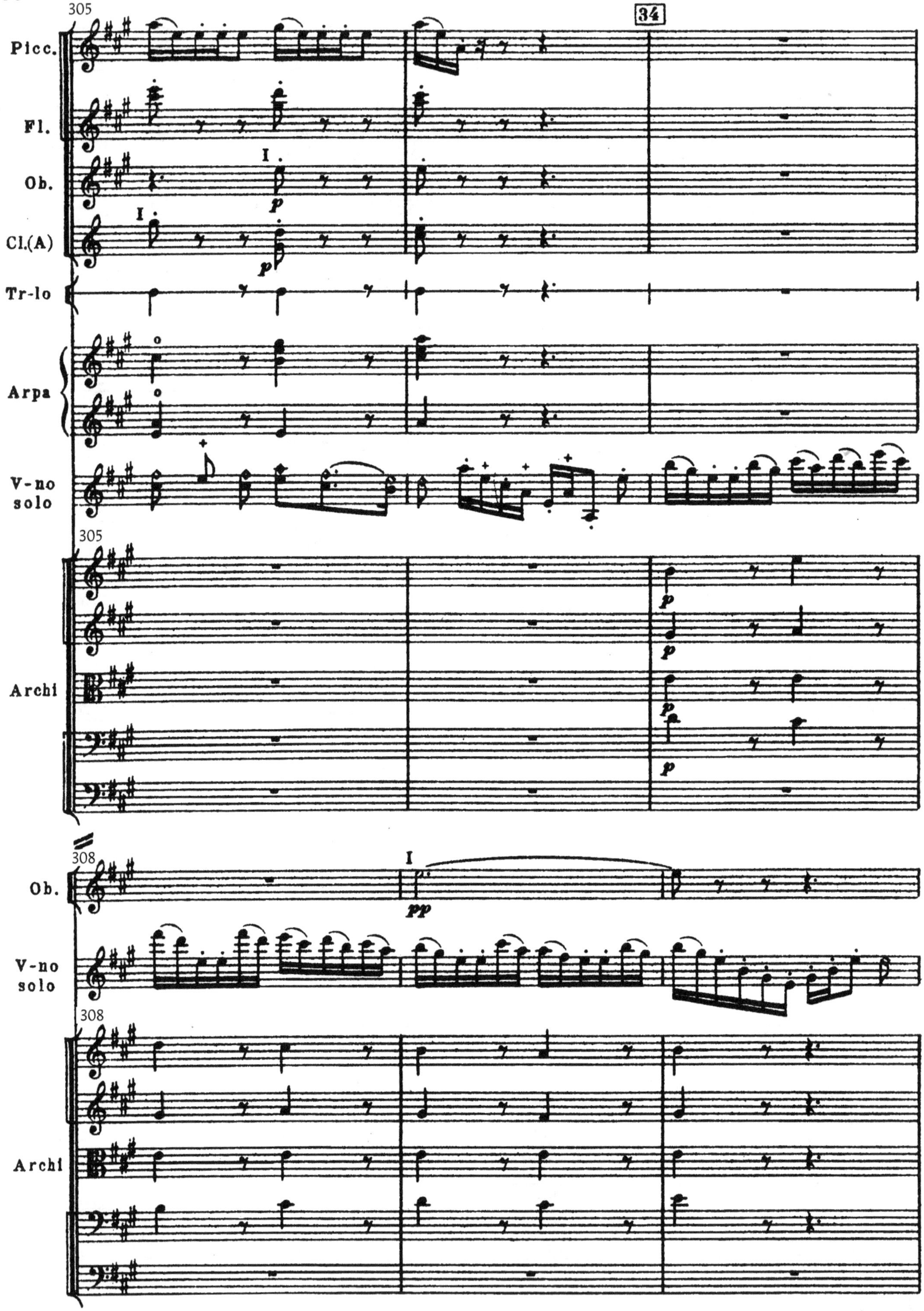
305
34
Picc.
Fl.
Ob.
Cl.(A)
Tr-lo
Arpa
V-no solo
Archi
308
I
p
pp

311
Picc.
p
Fl.
p
Ob.
I
Cl.(A)
p
Fag.
Cor.
Tr-be (A)
Tr-ni
Timp.
Tr-lo
Arpa
V-no solo
311
Archi

68

41397

318
Picc.
Fl.
Ob.
Cl.(A)
Fag.
Cor.
Tr-be (A)
Tr-ni
Timp.
V-no solo
p grazioso
318
unis.
div.
unis.
Archi
div.
unis.

323
36
Fag.
I
Cor.
p
V-no solo
323
pizz.
p
pizz.
Archi
p
pizz.
p
328
colla parte
37
a tempo
I
Fag.
p
cresc. poco
I
Cor.
V-no solo
a piacere
p
cresc.
328
dolce
cresc. poco
arco
pizz.
arco
mp
p cresc.
poco
arco
pizz.
arco
Archi
mp
p
arco
pizz.
mp
p
cresc. poco
pizz.
p
cresc. poco

334
Fl.
Ob.
Cl.(A)
Fag.
I
mf
p
Cor.
Tr-be
Tr-ni
Timp.
V-no
solo
f
mf
p
334
Archi
mf
mp
pp
arco
p
pizz.
p espr.

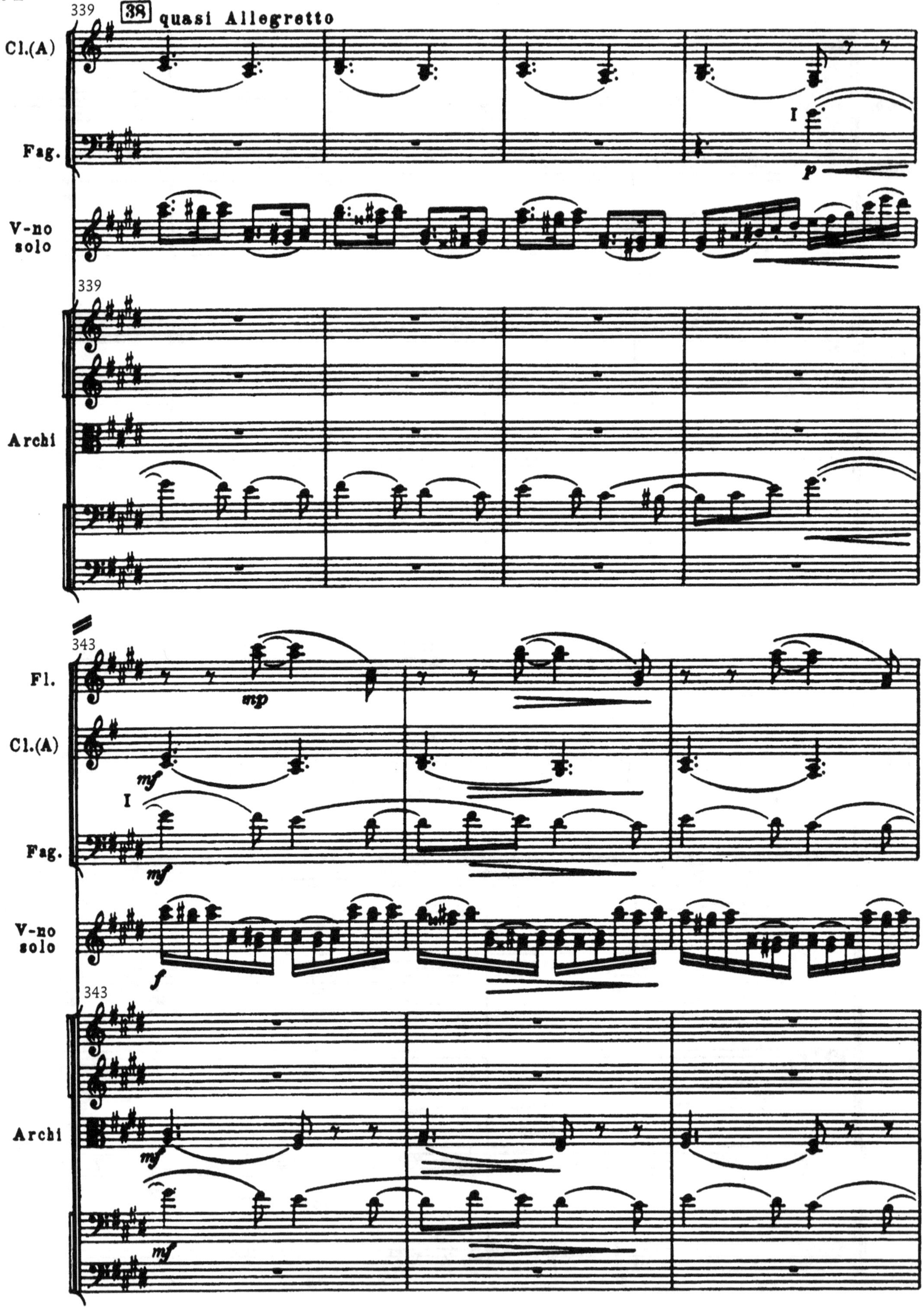
339
38
quasi Allegretto
Cl.(A)
Fag.
V-no solo
Archi
343
Fl.

346
39
animato poco
Fl.
Ob.
Cl.(A)
Fag.
Cor.
Tr-be (A)
Tr-ni
Timp.
Tr-lo
Arpa
V-no solo
animato poco
div pizz.
non div.
pizz.
div.
Archi

74

41397

352
Fl.
Ob.
Cl (A)
Fag.
Cor.
Tr-be
(A)
Tr-ni
Timp.
Tr-lo
V-no
solo
352
Archi
unis.

355
Fl.
Ob.
I
Cl.(A)
Fag.
Cor.
Tr-be
(A)
Tr-ni
Timp.
Tr-lo
V-no
solo
355
arco
arco
div.
arco
unis.
Archi
div.
arco
unis.
arco

357
40 Allegro
Fl.
Ob.
Cl.(A)
Fag.
Cor.
Tr-be (A)
Tr-ni
Timp.
V-no solo
357
40 Allegro
div.
div.
unis.
Archi

361
Fl.
Ob.
Cl.(A)
Fag.
Cor.
Tr-be (A)
Tr-ni
Timp.
V-no solo
f
361
unis.
Archi
div.

365
41
Fl.
Ob.
Cl.(A)
Fag.
mp
Cor.
Tr-be (A)
Tr-ni
Arpa
p
V-no solo
tr
Archi
div. pizz.
pizz.
mp

370
42
Fl.
Ob.
Cl.(A)
Fag.
Cor.
pp
Tr-be
(A)
Tr-ni
Arpa
V-no
solo
tr
p
370
42
unis.
pp
pizz.
pp
Archi

374
Fl.
Cl.(A)
I
p
III.IV
Cor.
Tr-lo
Arpa
V-no solo
tr
374
Archi
377
III.IV
Cor.
V-no
tr
377
Archi

380
43
Fl.
Ob.
Cl.(A)
Fag.
Cor.
a2
Tr-be (A)
Tr-ni
Tr-lo
Arpa
V-no solo
Archi
arco
pizz.
tr
f
mf
p
I

385
Fl.
I cantab.
Ob.
Cl.(A)
cantab.
Fag.
Cor.
III
Tr-be (A)
Tr-ni
Tr-lo
Arpa
V-no solo
385
Archi
tr
f
p
mf

389
44
Fl.
Ob.
Cl. (A)
Fag.
Cor.
Tr-be
Tr-ni
C-lli
Arpa
V-no solo
389
Archi
I
p
pp
tr

393
Fl.
Ob.
Cl.(A)
Fag.
Cor.
Tr-be (A)
Tr-ni
C-lli
Arpa
V-no solo
Archi
solo
tremolo
(pizz.) div
393

45
398
Fl.
Ob.
Cl.(A)
Fag.
Cor.
Tr-be (A)
Tr-ni
Tr-lo
Arpa
V-no solo
Archi
I solo
II
I
mp
pp
p
mf
div.
unis.
8

403
Fl.
Ob.
Cl. (A)
Fag.
Cor.
Tr-be (A)
Tr-ni
Tr-lo
Arpa
V-no solo
Archi
dolciss.
pp
mp
mf
div.
arco
I
8

407
46
Picc.
Fl.
cresc.
Ob.
Cl. (A)
Fag.
Cor.
Tr-be (A)
sole
Tr-ni
C-lli
Arpa
V-no solo
sul G
Archi

411
Picc.
Fl.
I
pp
Ob.
Cl.(A)
I
pp
Fag.
II
pp
Cor.
pp
III
pp
Tr-be (A)
Tr-ni
C-lli
Arpa
pp
V-no solo
411
unis. pizz.
pp
unis. pizz.
pp
Archi
pizz.
pp
pizz.
pp

417
47
animando poco a poco
Picc.
Fl.
Ob.
Cl. (A)
Fag.
Cor.
Tr-be (A)
Tr-ni
C-lli
Arpa
V-no solo
Archi
I
II
III
a2
cresc.
mf
arco

421
Picc.
Fl.
Ob.
Cl.(A)
Fag
Cor
a2
Tr-be (A)
Tr-ni
Arpa
V-no solo
p dolce
Archi
arco
div.

424
I
Ob.
Arpa
V-no
solo
mf
424
div.
V-le
p
V-c.
p
pizz.
C-b.
427
48
Picc.
p
II
Fl.
mp
I
p
I
Ob.
I
Cl (A)
mp
I
Cor.
p
Arpa
V-no
solo
p
427
V-le
pp
V-c.
pp
C-b.
pp

430
sempre animando
Picc.
Fl.
I
II
mf
Ob.
I
mp
Cl.(A)
p
Fag.
p
Cor
I
p
Tr-be (A)
Tr-ni
Arpa
p
V-no solo
430
sempre animando
Archi
p
p
p

433
49
più animato ♩.=138
II
I
Fl.
Ob.
Cl.(A)
Fag.
Cor.
Tr-be (A)
Tr-ni
Timp.
Arpa
V-no solo
433
49
più animato ♩.=138
pizz.
unis.
pizz.
pizz.
pizz.
Archi

437
Fl.
cresc.
Ob.
cresc.
Cl.(A)
cresc.
Fag.
cresc.
Cor.
cresc.
Tr-be (A)
Tr-ni
Timp.
cresc.
Arpa
cresc.
V-no solo
cresc.
437
Archi
cresc.
cresc.
cresc.
cresc.

441
50
Fl.
Ob.
Cl.(A)
Fag.
Cor.
Tr-be (A)
Tr-ni
Timp.
Tr-lo
P-tti
Arpa
V-no solo
Archi
I
f
mf
p
tr
arco
div.
arco

445
Fl.
Ob.
Cl.(A)
Fag.
Cor.
Tr-be (A)
I
f
Tr-ni
Timp.
Tr-lo
P-tti
Arpa
V-no solo
445
Archi

98

41397

455
52
Picc.
Fl.
Ob.
Cl.(A)
f
I
Fag.
f
Cor.
Tr-be (A)
Tr-ni
C-lli
Arpa
V-no solo
455
pizz.
52
f
pizz.
f
pizz.
f
pizz.
f
Archi

461
Picc.
Fl.
Ob.
Cl.(A)
Fag.
Cor.
Tr-be (A)
Tr-ni
C-lli
Arpa
V-no solo
461
Archi

467
53
Cl.(A)
Fag.
Tr-ni
V-no solo
V-ni I
V-ni II
V-le
V-c.
I
mp
arco
sul G
f pesante
p
pp
mf
arco
473
54
(sempre più animando)
solo
Cor.
Tr-lo
pizz.
mp

477
Fl.
Ob.
Cl.(A)
Fag.
Cor.
Tr-lo
V-no solo
V-ni I
V-ni II
V-le
a2
I
pizz.
arco
482
55
V-c.
cresc.

487
Cl.(A)
Fag.
Cor.
V-no solo
Archi
II
I solo
I
arco
cresc.
492
Fl.
Ob.
pizz.

497
56 ♩= 160
Fl.
Ob.
Cl.(A)
Fag.
Cor.
Tr-be (A)
Tr-ni
Tr-lo
Arpa
V-no solo
Archi
div.
non div.
pizz.
pizz. div.

501
Fl.
Ob.
Cl.(A)
Fag.
Cor.
Tr-be (A)
Tr-ni
Tr-lo
Arpa
V-no solo
501
div.
non div.
Archi

506
Fl.
Ob.
Cl.(A)
Fag.
a 2
Cor.
Tr-be (A)
Tr-ni
Timp.
Tr-lo
Arpa
V-no solo
cresc.
506
arco
non div.
Archi

511
57
a2
Fl.
Ob.
Cl.(A)
Fag.
Cor.
I
Tr-be (A)
Tr-ni
Timp.
Tr-lo
Arpa
V-no solo
Ossia:
div.
Archi

108

41397

521
58
Fl.
Ob.
Cl.(A)
Fag.
Cor.
Tr-be (A)
Tr-ni
Arpa
V-no solo
Archi
pizz.
pizz.
unis.
pizz.
pizz

525
Fag.
I
V-no solo
arco
unis.
Archi
529
Fag.
I
V-no solo
Archi
arco
arco

533
59 sempre animando
a2
Fl.
Ob.
Cl.(A)
Fag.
I
Cor.
Tr-be (A)
Tr-ni
Timp.
V-no solo
533
59 sempre animando
div.
Archi

537
Picc.
Fl.
Ob.
Cl.(A)
Fag.
Cor.
Tr-be (A)
Tr-ni
Timp.
Tr-lo
V-no solo
537
Archi
a2
II
I
tr
mf
dim.
p dim.
ff
pp
pizz.
6

541
60
Picc.
Fl.
tr
tr
Ob.
Cl.(A)
tr
tr
pp
Fag.
Cor
Tr-be
(A)
Tr-ni
Timp
tr
V-no
solo
p
541
60
pp
div.
pp
div.
unis.
p
pizz.
pp
div.
Archi
pp

546
61
Picc.
Fl.
Ob.
Cl.(A)
Fag.
Cor.
Tr-be
(A)
Tr-ni
Timp.
Tr-lo
V-no
solo
Archi
pp
cresc. poco
mp
I.
unis.
f
p

551
Fl.
I
Ob.
Cl.(A)
I
Fag.
p
Tr-lo
V-no
solo
551
Archi
pp
p
556
62
V-no
solo
556
Archi
pizz.
pp

561
Cl.(A)
Fag.
Cor.
V-no solo
Archi
III
pp
p cresc.
pp cresc.
cresc.
565
Tr-be (A)
I
f
cresc.
p
mf

569
63
Picc.
Fl.
Ob.
Cl.(A)
Fag.
Cor.
Tr-be (A)
I sola
Tr-ni
Timp.
Tr-lo
Arpa
V-no solo
Archi
arco
pizz.

576
Picc.
Fl.
a2
Ob.
Cl.(A)
Fag.
I
Cor.
a2
Tr-be (A)
I
Tr-ni
Timp.
Tr-lo
Arpa
V-no solo
Ossia:
arco
576
Archi
arco
div.
arco
arco
arco

581
64
Picc.
Fl.
Ob.
Cl.(A)
Fag.
Cor.
Tr-be (A)
Tr-ni
Timp.
Tr-lo
P-tti
C-lli
V-no solo
ossia:
Archi
mf cresc.
p cresc.